Discover the Lead
PIANO

Series Editor: Anna Joyce

Editorial, production and recording: Artemis Music Limited • Design and production: Space DPS Limited • Published 2001

IMP
International
MUSIC
Publications

Introduction

Welcome to DISCOVER THE LEAD, part of an instrumental series that provides beginners of all ages with fun, alternative material to increase their repertoire, but overall, enjoyment of their instrument!

For those of you just starting out, the idea of solo playing may sound rather daunting. DISCOVER THE LEAD will help you develop reading and playing skills, while increasing your confidence as a soloist.

You will find that the eight well-known songs have been carefully selected and arranged at an easy level - although interesting and musically satisfying. You will also notice that the arrangements can be used along with all the instruments in the series – flute, clarinet, alto saxophone, tenor saxophone, trumpet, violin and piano – making group playing possible!

The professionally recorded backing CD allows you to hear each song in two different ways:

- a complete demonstration performance with solo + backing
- backing only, so you can play along and DISCOVER THE LEAD!

Wherever possible we have simplified the more tricky rhythms and melodies, but if you are in any doubt listen to the complete performance tracks and follow the style of the players. Also, we have kept marks of expression to a minimum, but feel free to experiment with these – but above all, have fun!

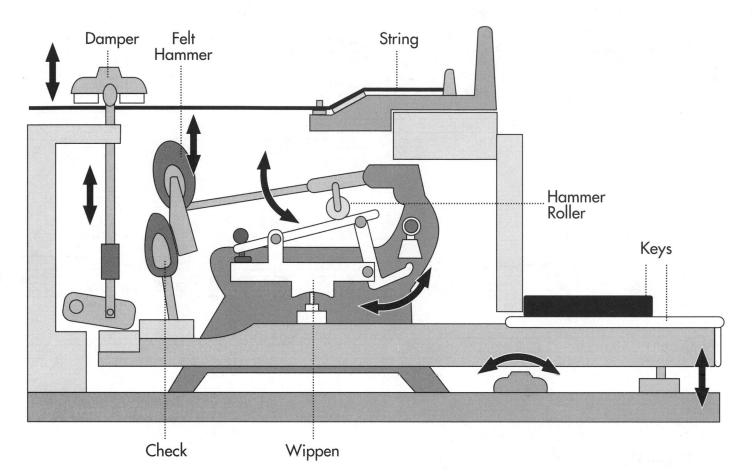

Damper

Felt
Hammer

String

Hammer
Roller

Keys

Check

Wippen

A piano relies on lever action that begins when a musician presses the keys. The piano's operating system, known as the action, and a key component, a metal wippen, control the sounding of the strings. The levers also raise and lower the dampers, devices that stop the strings vibrating and control the duration of the tone.

Ave Maria

Music by Franz Schubert

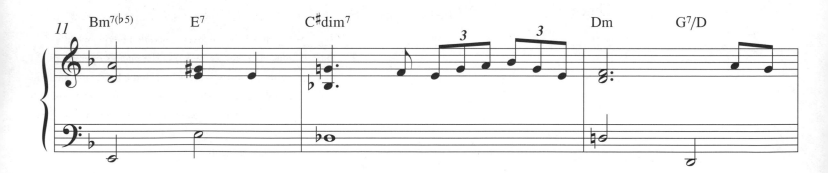

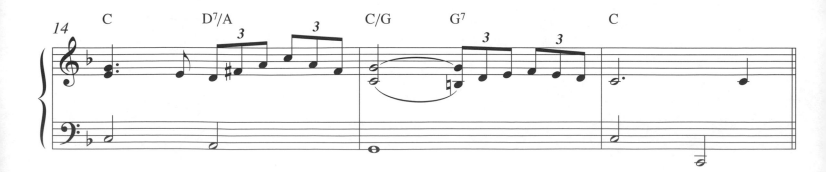

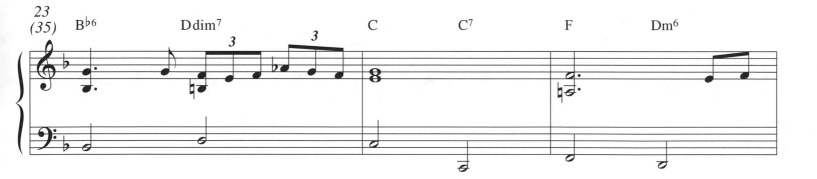

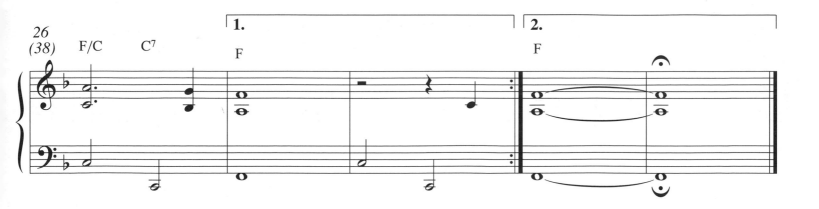

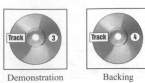

Demonstration   Backing

La Donna E Mobile
(from *Rigoletto*)

Music by Guiseppe Verdi

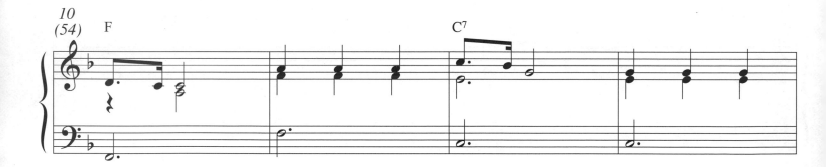

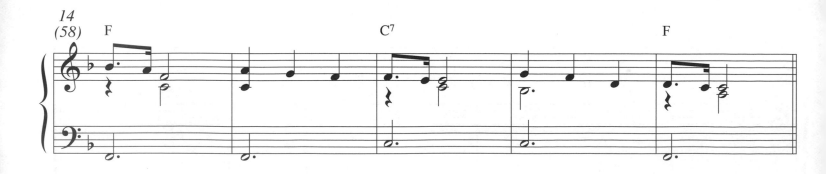

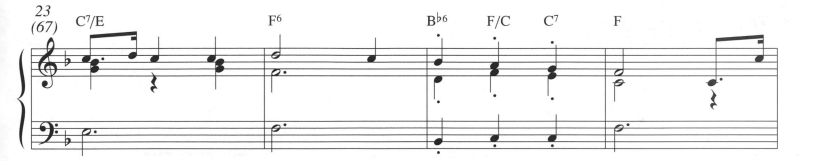

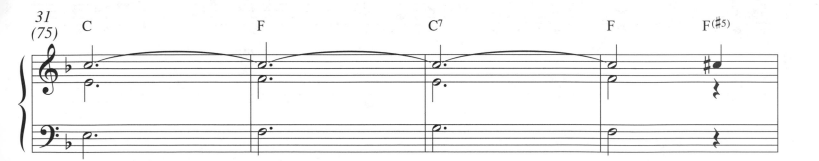

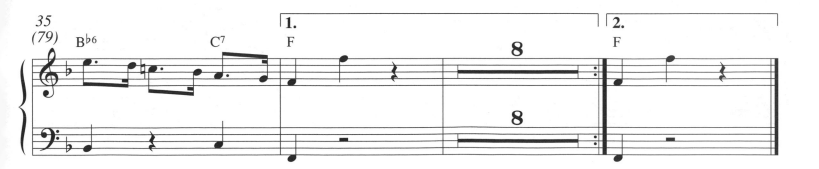

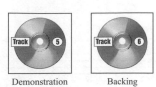

Demonstration   Backing

Largo
(from *New World Symphony*)

Music by Antonin Dvořák

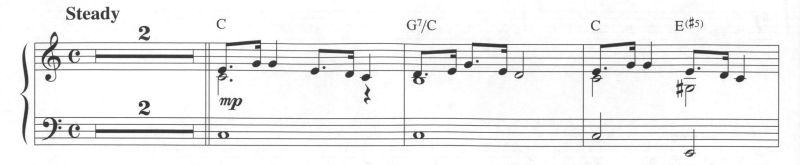

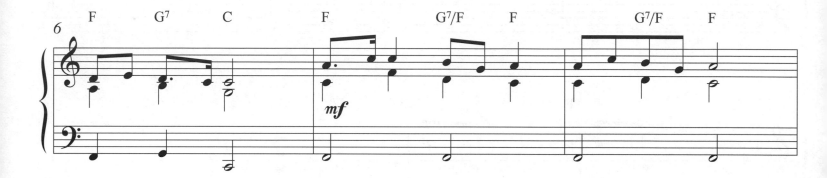

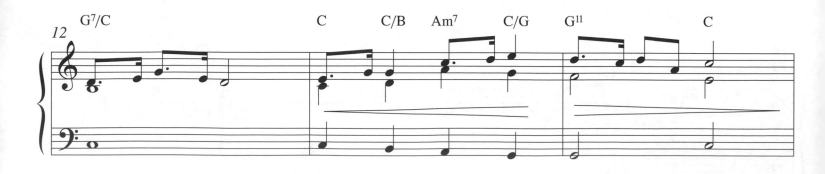

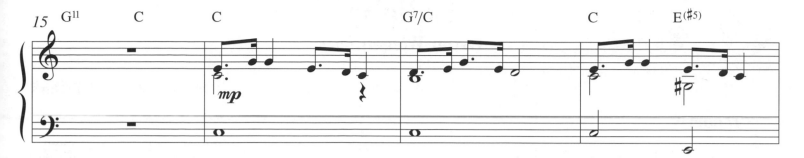

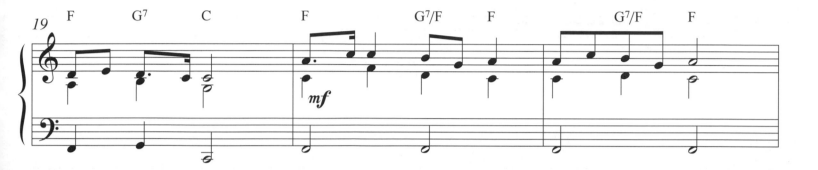

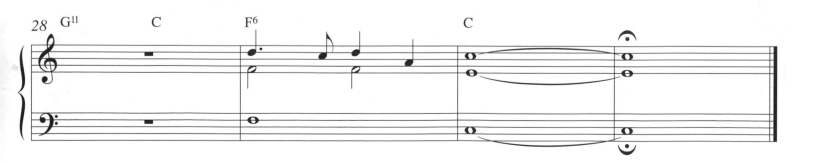

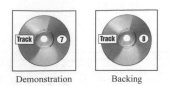

Demonstration   Backing

Lullaby
(from *Wiegenlied*)

Music by Johannes Brahms

Tenderly

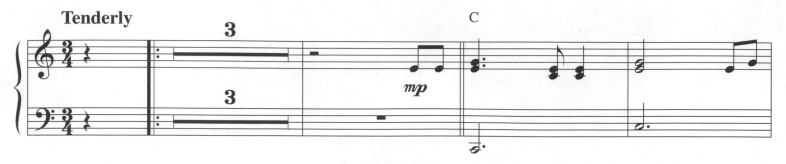

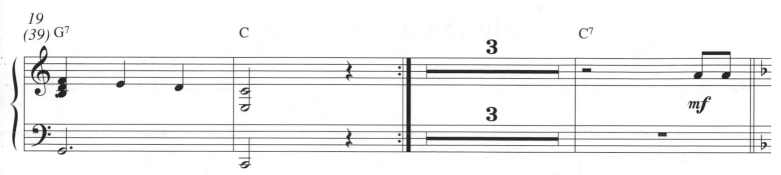

Air On A G String

Music by Johann Sebastian Bach

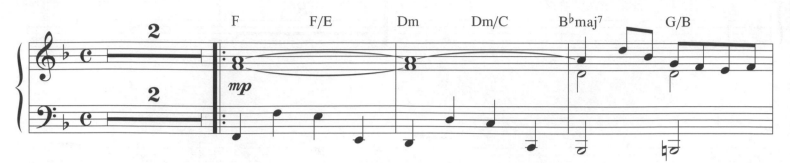

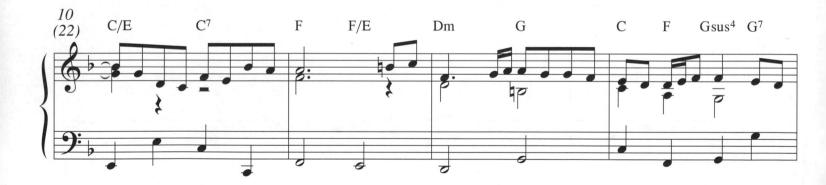

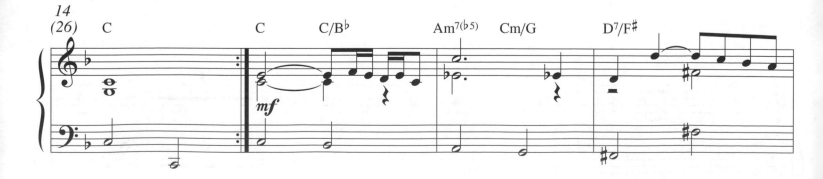

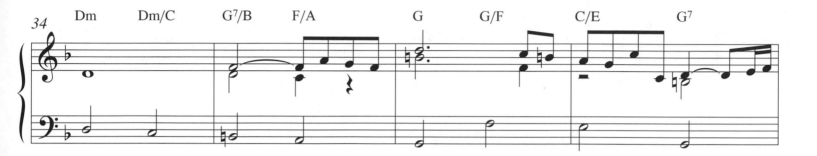

Morning
(from *Peer Gynt*)

Music by Edvard Grieg

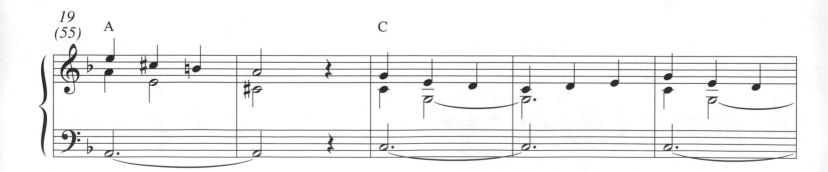

Demonstration   Backing

Ode To Joy
(from *Symphony No. 9*)

Music by Ludwig Van Beethoven

Allegro

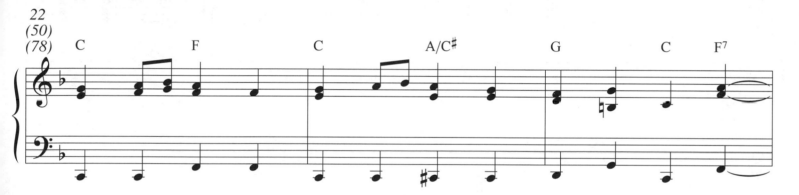

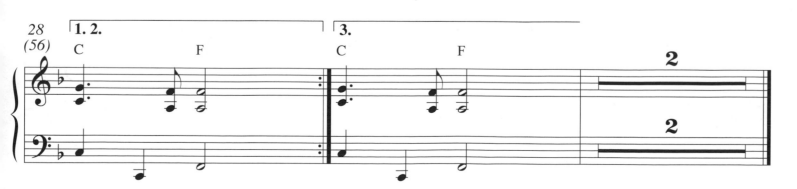

Spring
(from *The Four Seasons*)

Music by Antonio Vivaldi

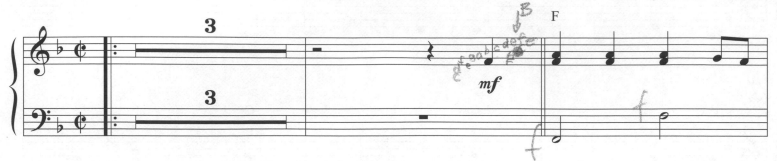

Printed in England by Halstan & Co. Ltd., Amersham, Bucks.

A Guide to Notation

Note and Rest Values

This chart shows the most commonly used note values and rests.

Name of note (UK)	Semibreve	Minim	Crotchet	Quaver	Semiquaver
Name of note (USA)	Whole note	Half note	Quarter note	Eighth note	Sixteenth note
Note symbol	o	♩	♩	♪	♪
Rest symbol	▬	▬	𝄽	𝄾	𝄿
Value per beats	4	2	1	1/2	1/4

Repeat Bars

When you come to a double dotted bar, you should repeat the music between the beginning of the piece and the repeat mark.

When you come to a repeat bar you should play again the music that is between the two dotted bars.

First, second and third endings

The first time through you should play the first ending until you see the repeat bar. Play the music again and skip the first time ending to play the second time ending, and so on.

D.C. (Da Capo)

When you come to this sign you should return to the beginning of the piece.

D.C. al Fine

When this sign appears, go back to the beginning and play through to the *Fine* ending marked. When playing a *D.C. al Fine*, you should ignore all repeat bars and first time endings.

D.S. (Dal Segno)

Go back to the 𝄋 sign.

D.S. al Fine

Go to the sign 𝄋 and play the ending labelled *(Fine)*.

D.S. al Coda

Repeat the music from the 𝄋 sign until the ⊕ or *To Coda* signs, and then go to the coda sign. Again, when playing through a *D. 𝄋 al Coda*, ignore all repeats and don't play the first time ending.

Accidentals

Flat ♭ - When a note has a flat sign before it, it should be played a semi tone lower.

Sharp ♯ - When a note has a sharp sign before it, it should be played a semi tone higher.

Natural ♮ - When a note has a natural sign before it, it usually indicates that a previous flat or sharp has been cancelled and that it should be played at it's actual pitch.

Bar Numbers

Bar numbers are used as a method of identification, usually as a point of reference in rehearsal. A bar may have more than one number if it is repeated within a piece.

Pause Sign

A pause is most commonly used to indicate that a note/chord should be extended in length at the player's discretion. It may also indicate a period of silence or the end of a piece.

Dynamic Markings

Dynamic markings show the volume at which certain notes or passages of music should be played. For example

pp	= very quiet	*mf*	= moderately loud
p	= quiet	*f*	= loud
mp	= moderately quiet	*ff*	= very loud

Time Signatures

Time signatures indicate the value of the notes and the number of beats in each bar.

The top number shows the number of beats in the bar and the bottom number shows the value of the note.